English learning via Boh Ramo Bokar Indigenous literature

Dr.*Nasi koje*

Dedicated to my first love children and youths of Boh Ramo Bokar.

One think that's close to my heart and absolutely breathtaking is the faces of the children and youths of the Boh Ramo Bokar community of Shi-Yomi District. Their faces remind me of a little girl from a small village filled with dreams and curiosity.

Preface

- To preserve and promote the culture of the *Boh Ramo Bokar* Communitiy of Shi Yomi District through learning second language (English).
- To bring culture into the classroom and rooting the *Boh Ramo Bokar* children with their ancestors.
- It brings culture into the ESL classroom as an educational function.
- It educates the *Boh Ramo Bokar* children about concern and responsibility towards the values of dialects and identity as a whole.
- Language preserves culture, the latter influences the language.
- It enhances the folklore and folkliterature of Boh Ramo Bokar Community.

Learning Four ESL Skills Through Boh Ramo Bokar Folkliterture

Volume-III

This section deals with the development of English Language book specially for the Boh Ramo Bokar children using folksongs and folktales collected and translated by the researcher. As in Volume-I and Volume-II, Boh Ramo Bokar folksongs and folktales are used to develop the English Language book three. Like Book-I and Book-II, the present Book-III also consist of five units arranged in a suitable order. Just as in Book-I and Book-II after every folksong and folktale there are activities developed by the researcher for the children. These activities are developed to enhanced the four English Language Skills: Listening, Reading, Speaking and Writing of the children. There are ten ESL activities. The activities are: **NEW WORDS, READING IS FUN, SAY ALOUD, LET'S WRITE, WORD BUILDING, TALK TIME, SONG TIME, TEAM TIME, PICTURE STORY,** and **PAPER FUN.**

CONTENTS

Unit-1

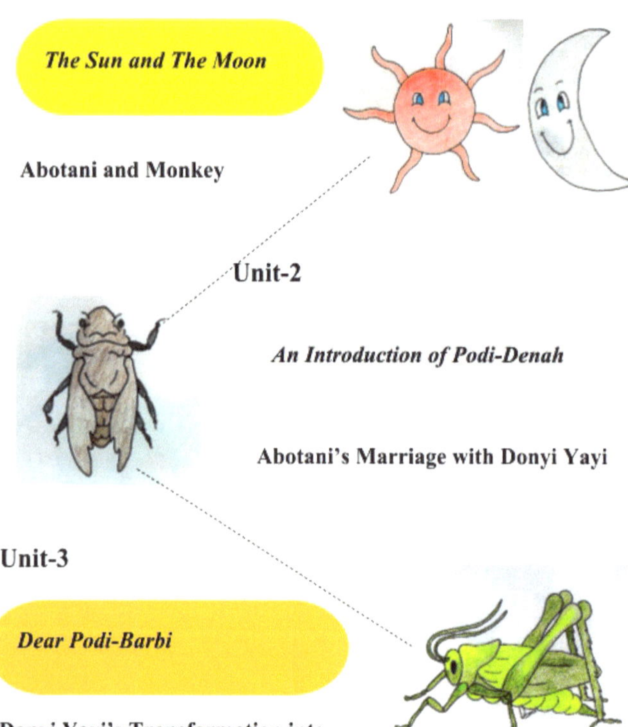

Unit-4

God of Fortune

Stupidity of Abotaro

Unit-5

Power of an Egg

Tani's Revenge

THE SUN AND THE MOON

Donyi means the Sun Jajinja,

Polo means the Moon Jajinja,

Donyi-Polo means the light Jajinja,

Donyi-Polo means the truth Jajinja,

Donyi-Polo means purity Jajinja,

Donyi-Polo means justice Jajinja,

Donyi-Polo means the wisdom Jajinja,

Donyi-Polo means the peace Jajinja,

Donyi-Polo means the love Jajinja,

Donyi-Polo means the hope Jajinja.

New words

Purity   Justice   Wisdom   Peace   Hope

Reading is fun

1) What is Donyi?

2) What is Polo?

3) What is meant by Donyi-Polo?

Talk time

1) What is the colour of Sun and Moon?

2) Do you know people worship Donyi-Polo?

3) Which people believe in Donyi-Polo?

Word building

1) Write the rhyming words of the following from the folksong -

   a) Notice _____________   b) Wood _______________

   c) Top _____________   c) Piece _______________

2) Write few lines about Sunrise and Sunset you wrote above.

____

____

____

Team time

Activity- Make a paper boat.

1. Start with an A4 sheet of paper. Fold in half, top to bottom.

2. To find centre, fold in the other direction and unfold.

3. Fold corners down using center fold as a guide.

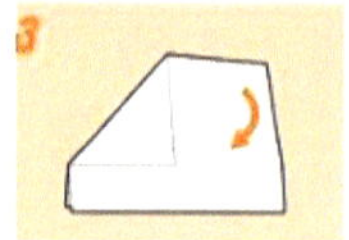

4. Fold flaps up on both sides.

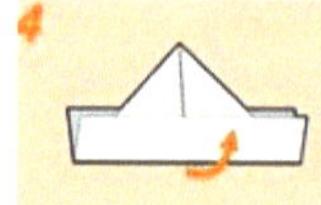

5. Put thumbs in middle and open out.

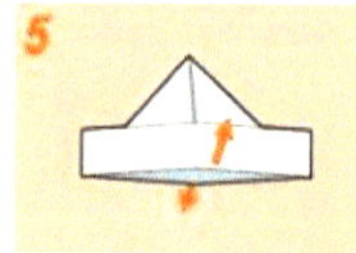

6. Until it makes a square. tuck corners of one flap under the other.

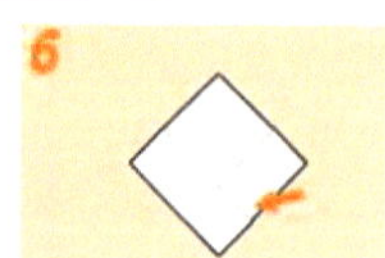

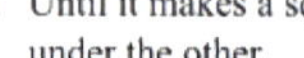

7. Fold up at both sides.

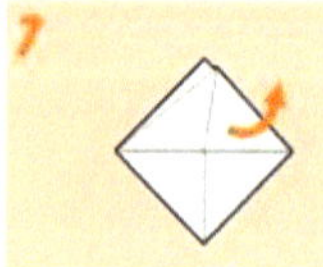

8. Put thumbs in middle and open out again.

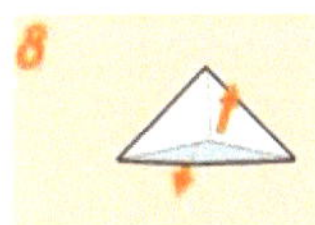

9. Until it makes a square. Pull corners out.

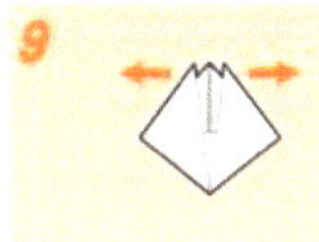

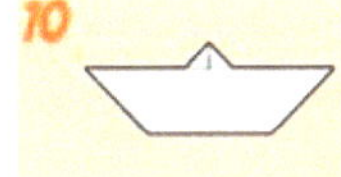

10. And press flat.

11. Open out to make boat shape.

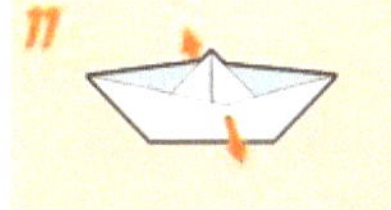

Song time

Donyi-Polo Donyi-Polo
Our Ane and Abo
Jajinja! Jajinja!
Ane Donyi is shining
Abo Polo is lighting
Jajinja! Jajinja!

ABOTANI AND MONKEY

In the ancient time the monkeys were considered to be more intelligent and superior than Abotani, Because the monkeys had bows, arrows, swords, machetes (locally known as daos). They were skilled at shooting, hitting, cutting, and jumping. Abotani felt inferior before them. He was jealous with monkey's advancements. Abotani thought 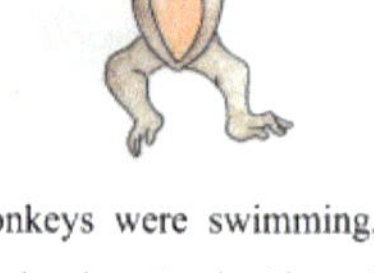 of an idea day and night to destroy the pride of monkeys.

One day when the monkeys were swimming, keeping their weapons on the river Bank, Abotani walked behind the monkeys, loosen the threads of the bows and tied them across each other. Later the monkeys started pushing, pulling and jerking each other because the threads were tied hard.

Gradually, the angry monkeys started to fight among themselves and threw the weapons. In this way the monkeys lost the skills of shooting. But the monkeys continued to damage the crop fields of Abotani which were the means of survival. So Abotani determined to destroy the dynasty of the monkeys.

One day Abotani dressed up himself in red costume, coloured red on his face, legs, hands, and roamed around the monkey's world. By looking at Abotani in new form, the monkeys also desired to have  same look. The greedy and curious monkeys requested him to help them for the transformation. Abotani accepted to help them, but in a condition that the monkeys have to follow certain rules.

Abotani advised the monkeys to collect a load of dry fire wood and gather them near the huge tree trunk. The monkeys happily followed the advice of Abotani and quickly loaded fire wood on the spot. Then Abotani advised all the monkeys to go inside the empty trunk. The excited monkeys with ambition to have good colour and beauty rushed into the tree trunk. When all the monkeys went inside the empty trunk, Abotani slowly tightly closed the entrance of the trunk by the dry firewood. Abotani advised, when they turn red utter the words, "oh! Abotani, we turned red." The monkeys were still so happy and prolong to follow his advice. After that, Abotani set the dry wood on fire and deadly flames gutted down the monkeys. The monkeys were crying loudly uttering the words, "Abotani we turned red". But Abotani continued to blow the fire till all monkeys became silent.

After setting off the fire, Abotani brought out the dead bodies of monkeys counting one by one. Later one injured young female monkey jumped out. She was alive inside the dead bodies of other monkeys. She ran away into the forest and climbed into the top of the tree. It is believed that from the very day, the monkeys face turns black, its bottom red and lived on trees forever. Abotani could not destroy the empire of the monkeys. That's why the monkeys still exist on the earth.

Moral: *The above folktale shows the relationship of human and animal. It pictures how nature has played an important role in shaping their lives. The animals also act like the human; they can do all activities which are done by the human. This folktale has importance in Boh Ramo Bokar community because the folktale gives lessons to the youths and children. Through this folktale we can know the activeness of the monkeys and why they stay in the trees only. The moral of the story is the too much torturing to anyone can harm their life and family.*

New words

Machetes Entrance Pride Empire Superior Jerk Determined Dynasty Curious

Reading is fun

1. In ancient times who were considered to be more intelligent?

2. Why were monkeys considered to be superior to Abotani?

3. How many monkeys jumped out of the fire?

4. How did Abotani get rid of the monkeys?

5. What is the moral of the story?

Talk time

Monkeys

Monkey is an animal.

Monkeys are of different colours red, brown, white.

Monkey likes to climb trees.

Monkeys love to eat bananas.

Monkeys jump from branches to branches of trees.

Monkeys stay in group and play with each other.

1. Have you ever seen monkeys before?

2. What are the colours of monkeys?

Say aloud

Jealous   Curious   Dangerous
Pushing   Pulling   Jerking
Fire   Desire   Liar

Team time

Activity - Make a set of an arrow and bow using bamboo.

Word building

1) Fill in the blanks in the given shape with their opposite words

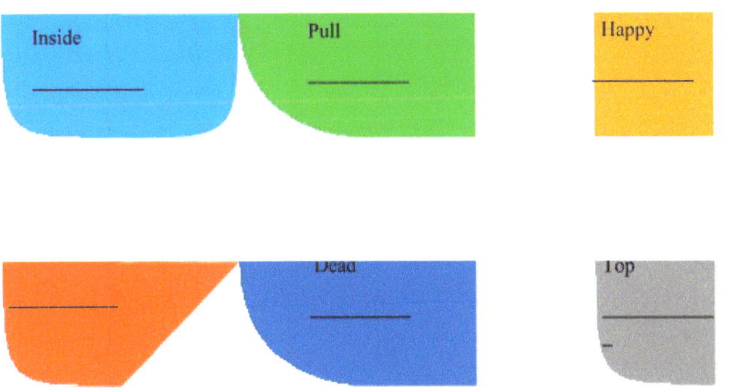

Let's write 

Write four sentences on riverside using the followings words:

trees   monkey   chirp   fly   sky

____

____

____

____

Teacher's Page____ UNIT I

This section is for the teacher. It is to be used as a reference for teaching and motivating students. This page will give the brief highlight of the unit and activities and suggestions to be followed as much as you can. This page is highly recommended for teacher to use while teaching the class.

THEMES

- Meaning of the sun and the moon in tribal life.
- Relationship of human and animal.
- Natures role in shaping their lives.

SUGGESTIONS FOR CLASSROOM TEACHING

- To introduce the theme and mood of the folksong firstly read the pre-reading questions aloud. Read the folksong aloud with appropriate hand motion and actions.
- Ask the children describe the picture in the folksong.
- Read the folktale in audible voice slowly and with gestures.
- Motivate and ask the children to look at the book as you read it. After you have done reading it ask the students to read it two lines each consecutively aloud till the reading of the folktale is over such that let the next student read from the sentence where the previous student stopped. This repeated reading will help the child to understand the language along with learning to read.

FOR TEAM TIME

- Make groups of children with equal numbers of children in each group. The song "Donyi-Polo" can be continued by adding lines like

"Donyi- Polo Donyi-Polo

Please Don't Go away

When Rain Comes

Donyi-Polo Donyi-Polo

Help me to shine like you in life

And enlighten people with knowledge and happiness."

- Children can start a star gazing at night and collect various information about it from the sources available. This activity can continue till the next full moon.
- Assist and Encourage children to make the bamboo craft. Help them in collecting bamboo and cutting it and lastly instruct them in making the craft mentioned in the activity. Also help them in making other bamboo crafts like bamboo basket, bamboo pot etc.

- Encourage children to make paper crafts. Ask the children to bring colour papers. Instruct and join with children during the process. After completion paste it on the note book.
- Make use of blackboard to put down new words. Ask children to have a notebook for new words. Develop the habit and practice of making fair and rough notebook in children to note down the new words, answers and other activities.
- Ask children to start making a chart of New Words and compile it later after the completion of all unit. Put up new words from each units each week on the chart. This will give the collection of all new words they have learned from the book in one chart.
- With the progresses in activity, you can start preparing for other charts to accommodate word-families like adjectives, adverbs, nouns, prefixes and suffixes. Also, can put up tenses, opposites and much more as this will help in increase of vocabulary in the children.

AN INTRODUCTION OF PODI-DENAH

Podi-Denah Jajinja,

Let me introduce you to Podi-Denah Jajinja,

Podi-Denah is a cricket like insect Jajinja,

Podi-Denah is an insect named Cicada Jajinja,

Podi-Denah lives in a high mountain Jajinja,

Podi-Denah makes melodious noise Jajinja,

Podi-Denah's noise brings good news Jajinja,

Podi-Denah's noise brings bad news Jajinja,

Our Podi-Denah is special Jajinja,

Podi-Denah Jajinja.

New words

Introduce   Melodious   Cricket   Special

Reading is fun

1) What is Podi-Denah?

2) Where does Podi-Denah live?

3) How is Podi-Denah's noise?

4) What kind of news does Podi-Denah bring?

Talk time

1) What do you call cicada in your native language?

2) Find out what is the importance of cicada insect.

3) What kind of insects are edible?

Team time

Activity – Let's make Insect finger puppet.

i.   Draw your favourite insect on a sheet of paper, cut and colour it.

ii.   Take a strip of cloth or paper.

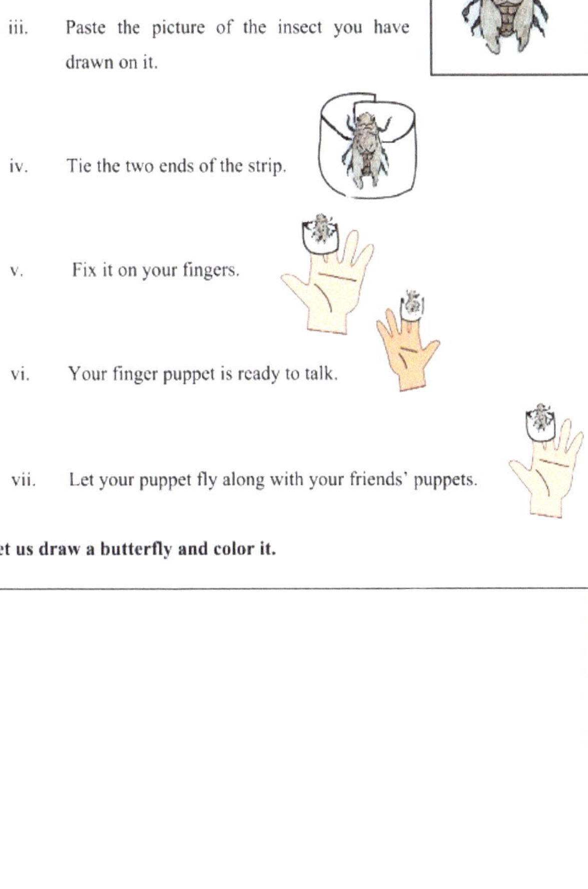

iii.   Paste the picture of the insect you have drawn on it.

iv.   Tie the two ends of the strip.

v.   Fix it on your fingers.

vi.   Your finger puppet is ready to talk.

vii.   Let your puppet fly along with your friends' puppets.

Let us draw a butterfly and color it.

 **Let's write** 

Listen to the sounds of the insects. Make a list of these words.

For example: Buzz   Buzz   Buzz

____

____

Now write four sentences on insects using the followings words.

chirp	buzz	squeak	drone	wings	glide	sing	noise

____

____

____

____

Say aloud 

High Low

Good Bad

Melodious Unmelodious

ABOTANI'S MARRIAGE WITH DONYI YAYI

Once upon a time, Abotani visited the land of Donyi-polo which was known for the beauty and beautiful girls. Abotani had a strong rod. Abotani challenged them "Who is the strongest among the girls to break my rod?" Dongnyi Yayi jumped out from a metal container and broke his rod. He proposed her for marriage, but she refused to marry Abotani. In order to win her heart, Abotani lied that he is the richest man of earth. His palace is made up of gold and silver. At last, Dongnyi Yayi agreed to go with him.

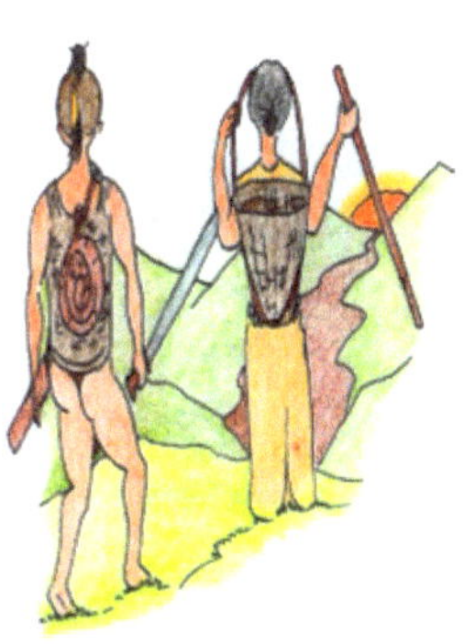

The journey to earth was quite long and tough. On the way she came across many palaces but Abotani kept saying his palace is much more superior than all. Finally, they landed in a small hut surrounded by bushes, creepers and trees. Chickens and puppies welcomed and served her food. They were the only family of Abotani. Dongnyi Yayi was very unhappy with the fact.

But due to heavy work and cultivation she became weak. She requested Abotani to inform her health condition to her parents. Abotani visited her parent's house and

told the condition about her sickness. While returning they gave him a packed green leaf and warned him not to open on the way. Curious Abotani did not follow the advice and opened the packed leave, and was shocked to see a dead body of a baby and a knife.

She ate the packet leave send by her parents, and became healthy, beautiful and pregnant. Abotani told her that he was going to forest to manage rope for the baby. She permitted him to go and warned him to be careful about the devils on the way. She gave birth to two sons but Abotani never returned.

Moral: *The moral of the story is that a lady should be humble, supportive and hardworking like Dongnyi Yayi.*

New words

Superior   Creepers   Humble   Advice   Rod

Reading is fun

1) Which land is known for beauty and beautiful girls?

2) Who did break Abotani's rod?

3) What was in the packet sent by Dongyi Yayi's parents?

4) What did Abotani lie to Dongyi Yayi?

Talk time

1. Have you ever been to forest before?

2. How many brothers and sisters do you have?

3. Have you ever been to paddy filed?

Picture story

Number the jumbled lines story correctly. Then write the story in proper order.

And then they shared the food.

Once there was a Tame the ant and Takar the grasshopper.

Tame said "Let's eat the food."

On its way back to home after collecting food from forest Tame met Takar.

Tame ask "How are You Takar ?" Takar replied "I am fine, thank you!"

Write the aforementioned story here.

____

____

____

____

____

Team time

1) Do you like pets? If so, which is your favourite pet.

2) Try making a picture and list of items such as foods of your favourite pet.

3) Share the name of your favourite pet with friends.

4) Collect different colours of feathers of birds without hurting them and paste on your note book and write a few lines about them.

Word building

1. Fill in the blanks with correct letters to spell words from the story.

Ch _ _ _ _ _ ged

C _ _t_ _n_r

M _ _r_ _g_

R _ _h_ _t

Jo_ rn _ _

S _pe _ _ _r

Cr _ _pe _ _

C _ _ti_at_ _n

S _ _k_ _ _s

B _ _ _ti _ _ _

2. Write similar words from the story:

Difficult	_________	Reject	_________
Senior	_________	Circumstances	_________
Depart	_________	Supervise	_________

3. Fill in the blanks with suitable words from the folktale.

1) _________ jumped out of the metal container.

2) Abotani visited the land of _________.

3) Due to heavy work and cultivation Dongyi Yayi became _________.

4) _________ and _________ welcome and served Dongyi Yayi food.

Say aloud

Strong   Weak   Rod   Curious   Heavy

Strange   Week   Rot   Cute   Head

Teacher's Page____ UNIT II

THEMES

- Cicada
- Changes and responsibilities in life of a lady before and after marriage

SUGGESTIONS FOR CLASSROOM TEACHING

- Just like Unit-1 read the pre-reading questions aloud to introduce the theme or topic of the folksong to warm up.
- Read the folksong aloud laying stress on certain words along with expression.
- Take children for a walk around the nearest jungle or trees. Let them search for insects and point it out without touching it as they may see on the trees or plants. Encourage them to look and observe for various insects around them and listen attentively to their sounds. Ask the children about their thoughts and feelings.
- Talk about differences between different kinds of insects, e.g. in size, shape, move, eat, colour, sounds etc. Teach them about their importance, beauty and encourage them to preserve insects.
- Read the folktale aloud to the children in the class along with the help of the pictures. Ask children to guess the meanings of difficult words before you explain this will build confidence.
- Take children to the nearest jungle and farm or local pet store and zoo for the insect activity. Assist and make finger puppet apart from showing them how to make finger puppet before that explain the position names of the fingers to children. After the completion of making of finger puppet encourage theme - based conversation amongst the children
- Discuss with children how insects evolved and what roles they play in maintaining the balance of our nature. What would happen if there were no insects?

DEAR PODI-BARBI

Podi-Barbi, Podi-Barbi Jajinja,

Migrates from far of place Jajinja,

Podi-Barbi, Podi-Barbi Jajinja,

Migrates at season of harvesting Jajinja,

Podi-Barbi, Podi-Barbi Jajinja,

Celebrated to welcome harvesting Jajinja,

Podi-Brabi, Podi-Barbi Jajinja,

Celebrated to thanks mother nature Jajinja,

Podi-Barbi, Podi-Barbi Jajinja,

Perform in every year Jajinja,

Podi-Parbi, Podi-Barbi Jajinja,

Perform will never end Jajinja.

New words

Migrates   Season   Celebrated   Harvesting   Perform

Reading is fun

1) What is a Podi-Barbi?

2) Where did Podi-Barbi migrate from?

3) Why is Podi-Barbi celebrated?

4) Will Podi-Barbi ever end?

Talk time

1) Which festival do you celebrate in your tribe?

2) Write the names of food that you prepare during your festival.

Let's write

1) Write the meaning of following words using dictionary

Migrates   _______________________________________

Harvesting   _______________________________________

Celebrate   _______________________________________

Perform   _______________________________________

2) Name the four seasons of a year.

   i)   ________________

   ii)   ________________

   iii)   ________________

   iv)   ________________

3) Fill in the blanks with right word from the box

Si-Donyi	Losar	Loku	Boori-Boot
Nyokum-Yullo	Solung	Mopin	Dree

   i.   Adi tribe celebrates _________ festival.

   ii.   Apatani tribe celebrates _________ festival.

   iii.   Nyishi tribe celebrates _________ festival.

   iv.   Tagin tribe celebrates _________ festival.

   v.   Galo tribe celebrates _________ festival.

   vi.   Monpa tribe celebrates _________ festival.

   vii.   Hill-Miris tribe celebrates _________ festival.

   viii.   Nocte tribe celebrates _________ festival.

DONYI YAYI'S TRANSFORMATION INTO SUNRAYS

Long ago Dongnyi Yayi with her twin son was very unhappy because her husband Abotani did not return back from the forest. She waited for him for many years. So, she decided to go back to her parent's house. She was sorrowful and sad at home. So, she asked her sons to bring water from the stream.

She stood near fire place. The boys asked mother 'What are you doing?" She replied, "I am repairing your father's fire place made up of metal." She ordered the boys to bring water for the second time standing beside square shape rack for storing foods and firewood. The boys again asked their mother "What are you doing now?" She replied "I am maintaining your father's rack made up of expensive swords." Third time she asked to fetch water standing nearby by basement.

The boys asked mother "What you are doing now?" She replied I am repairing the basement of your father's house made up of swords. She told the boys to continue fetching water from the stream. They found their mother on the ceiling. They asked mother

"What are you doing?" now she replied "I am renovating your father's silver ceiling."

Again, she ordered her sons to bring water from the stream. They went and arrived home with water. They found their mother at the roof of the house. They asked mother "What are you doing now?" She replied "I am maintaining your father's golden roof." Again, she ordered her sons to bring water from the stream. They went and came back with water at home. This time they found their mother within the rays of sun.

Moral: *This tale educates the Boh Ramo Bokar youths about the deep relationship between human and nature.*

New words

Sorrowful   Expensive   Renovating   Stream   Metal   Fetch   Rays

Reading is fun

1) Why was Dongyi Yai unhappy?

2) What did Dongyi Yai told her sons to bring?

3) What was Dongyi Yai doing?

4) What happened to Dongyi Yai at the end?

Talk time

1) Have you ever seen a twin before?

2) Do you have a twin?

3) What would you like to talk about if you had a twin?

4) Have you ever gathered firewood from the jungle?

Team time

1) Make a group of four.

2) Collect a flowering plant and plant them in a pot.

3) Take care of it daily.

Let's write

Fill in the blanks with right words from the story.

1) Dongyi Yayi was unhappy because Abotani did not return from _______.

2) She asked her son to bring __________ from__________.

3) "I am repairing your father's fire place made of__________", she said.

4) The sons found their mother within the _______ of sun.

Say aloud

Forest Rarerest

Firewoods foods

Basement Sentiment

Fetching Maintaining

Teacher's Page________________________________ UNIT III

THEMES

- Podi-Barbi's importance and harvest
- Relationship between human and nature for their existence

SUGGESTIONS FOR CLASSROOM TEACHING

- Read the folksong aloud with expression so that children pay attention and enjoy the folksong. After the completion of unit let the children recite the folksong.

- Assist and instruct the children with the materials for the flower planting activity. You can use empty plastic cold drink bottles or bamboo as pots for flower planting that way children will learn to preserve the environment.

- Discuss the importance of stream for the peoples leaving in the hilly area and preserving it. Ask the children to help you make a list of ideas and harvesting festivals for it on the blackboard.

- You can also emphasise on how they can keep the stream and their surrounding clean to make it free from pollution.

- Let the class talk about relation between the flowers and insects. Let them talk and collection information how stream water helps in cultivation of crops. Let them imagine what would happen if there were no streams.

- Read out the folktale in an enjoyable manner to attract the children's attention. In telling the folktale involve the child to participate such as by asking interesting questions about the folktale and that way they actively participate, and enjoy the text and is certain that success will follow.

- Ask for volunteers from children to act the folktale. Let the children use their own words to make a new sentence in that way they will gain experience and add life and meaning.

- Tell the class about seasons of a year and its change that we observe around us like falling down of old leaves, growing new leaves. You could ask the children about changes they see in different seasons around them and note it down. This can help them in the writing activity.

- Also always motivate children to guess the meanings of difficult words, before you explain them as you read the folksong and folktale.
- Also Discuss about the various festivals celebrated by different tribes in Arunachal Pradesh and their significance.

GOD OF FORTUNE

We are waiting for Gunte-Gomteh Jajinja,

The God of fortune Jajinja,

We are waiting for your arrival Jajinja,

We are waiting for your sweet sound Jajinja,

We are waiting for your blessings Jajinja,

We are waiting for your love Jajinja,

We are waiting for your goodness Jajinja,

We are waiting for your support Jajinja,

We are waiting for happiness Jajinja,

We are waiting for Gunte-Gomteh Jajinja,

New words

Waiting   Fortune   Arrival   Blessings   Goodness

Reading is fun

1) Who is Gunte-Gomteh?

2) Why are people waiting for Gunte-Gomteh?

3) What does Gunte-Gomteh bring along with her?

Word building

1) Write the opposite words of the following

Fortune _________	Sweet _________
Love _________	happiness _________
Good _________	

2) Write the rhyming words of the following

Fortune _________	Sweet _________
Love _________	happiness _________
Good _________	

Let's write

Look! Look!

There is the secret island

The island filled with treasure

Finally, we have found it.

Let's find the boat to reach the island

But it will tough.

Choose the right words.

1. There is the ______ island. (popular/secret).

2. The island filled with ______ (waste/treasure).

3. But it will ______ (tough/Easy).

Say aloud

Peter Piper picked a peck of pickled peppers

A peck of pickled peppers Peter Piper picked

If Peter Piper picked a peck of pickled peppers

Where's the peck of pickled peppers Peter Piper picked?

Read the following

Health   Wealth

God   Almighty

Happiness   Cheerfulness

STUPIDITY OF ABOTARO

In the olden days there were two brothers Abotani and Abotaro. Abotani was more active, clever and used to dominate Abotaro in every situation. One day both brothers went to forest to hunt mouse using a special flat stone. They returned home after three days making instrumental traps to kill mouse.

Abotani visited the forest on the eve of second night, collected all the mouse trapped by Abotaro and secretly returned home. On

third day Abotani

again joins Abotaro to check the trapped mouse but there was not a single mouse. Abotaro tried hunting the mouse again and again for many months, but it resulted with failure and disappointment. He was not aware that Abotani is fooling him.

One day he asked Abotani, "What instrument do you use to trap the mouse?" Abotani replied, "I am using pork as a harpoon to hunt mouse." Abotaro was very impressed with his idea. He killed his pig, cut into pieces and used as harpoon. Abotani have been waiting for an opportunity to fool Abotaro. Abotani visited the forest in the same night. He collected all the pork meat from Abotaro's trap. Then he secretly returned home, had pork dinner with his family.

The family members used the fatty part of pork as their face cream. Next morning Abotaro visited Tani's house, and was impressed with shinny skin of Tani's family. Taro requested him to share the secret behind the beautiful skins of his family members so that he can apply the same idea.

Tani invited Taro for pork dinner. Abotani advised him to make a big bamboo container, and cover with thick clothe. Next, he has to insert his family members inside

the containers, closed tightly and pour boiled water from top of the container again and again. After three days he has to remove the cover of the container, and he will find his family members with fair skin. After three days a cock of Abotaro informed him about the transformation of his family into rotten worms. Abotaro turned crazy because he thought that the cock was cursing his family, and chop the cock into pieces. But later Taro found only bones and worms of his family. Abotaro got paranoid and revengeful.

Moral: *The moral of the tale is that one should have tremendous faith and not imitate others. It also educates us not to trust anyone easily and have faith in one's skill.*

New words

Dominate, Instruments, Trap, Paranoid, Transform, Curse, Disappointment, Tremendous, Imitate, Revengeful.

Reading is fun

1) Who was more active and cleverer among Abotani and Abotaro?

2) What did Abotani lie about his hunting techniques?

3) What did Abotaro do after hearing Abotani's hunting technique?

4) Why were Abotaro turned crazy and what did he do to the cock?

5) What is the moral of the story?

Talk time

1) How would you feel if you were Abotaro?

2) How much do you love your brothers and sisters?

3) Have you ever been to forest?

4) What kind of animals and birds you have seen in the forest?

Word Building

Look at the pattern and fill in the blanks one is done:

Great	**Greater**		
Brave	__________	Dense	__________
Brief	__________	Dark	__________
Fair	__________	Fine	__________

Fill in the blanks with the right word from the box.

sloth	band	nest	flock	drift

1) A group of mice is called a __________

2) A group of pigs is called a __________

3) A group of chicken is called a __________

4) A group of men is called a __________

5) A group of bears is called a __________

Let's write

Visit the nearest jungle or forest. Write five sentences on whatever you see.

____

____

____

____

Say aloud

Boomerang	Crossbow	Catapult	Axe	Spear	Harpoon

Song time

Abotani and Mouse

Abotani! Abotani!

Please don't kill me.

I will share my food with you.

We can be friends forever.

And help each other.

Teacher's Page____ UNIT IV

THEMES

- The God of Fortune
- Importance of trust and faith in oneself.

SUGGESTIONS FOR CLASSROOM TEACHING

- Read the poem aloud with appropriate action and gesture. After that motivate the children to recite the poem with appropriate actions and gestures.

- Assist and encourage the children to find rhyming words and opposites.

- Keep explaining the difficult words in the text during the reading process.

- Ask and encourage the children try to say the tongue twister (Peter Piper picked a peck...) aloud and as clearly as they can. Apart from that they can also try some other tongue twister like Betty Botter bought some butter, how can a clam cram in a clean cream can? etc. can be said quite slowly at first and the speed up later.

- Read the folktale aloud with suitable expression and gestures. As you read give the children ideas and opportunities to express themselves. Let the children enjoy the word by turning it into a suitable game as children practice correct pronunciation and build up words.

- Let the children to make different sounds of animals and birds.

- You can talk various hunting techniques followed by the ancient peoples. Discuss about the good and bad effect of hunting in the environment. Let them talk and express their ideas and knowledge about hunting. Encourage them in the preserving of wildlife.

- Ask the children whether they have eaten meat gathered from hunting and their experience. Talk about the importance of wildlife and share information about wildlife found in there.

- This unit can introduce the importance of self-belief and faith.

POWER OF AN EGG

This is the story of a power of an egg Jajinja,

An Egg is considered as very powerful Jajinja,

An Egg is the angel of God Jajinja,

An Egg cannot be harmed by devils' power Jajinja,

An Egg has the power to talk to God Jajinja,

An Egg speaks with human beings Jajinja,

An Egg cannot be harmed by the heat of a fire Jajinja,

An Egg cannot be destroyed by heat of a water Jajinja,

Jajinja the powerful Egg.

New words

Considered Speak Harm Heat Destroyed

Reading is fun

1) What is this poem about?

2) Can egg be destroyed by the heat of water?

3) Why is egg in this poem considered to be powerful?

Talk time

1) Do think of egg as same as you thought earlier?

2) Do you like to eat Egg?

3) How many eggs can you eat at a time?

4) What do you call egg in your language? Share it.

5) Why do you think egg can talk to God?

Let's Write

Write three sentences about an egg.

i) ____________________________________

ii) ___________________________________

iii) __________________________________

Say aloud

Angel   Individual   Emotional

Devil   Ill   Bill

Paper fun

Activity- Build a bird nest

Materials:

1. One brown paper lunch bag per student

2. Assorted sticks, leaves, etc.

3. A real bird nest or photos of bird nests

4. Craft clue

5. Optional:

> craft feathers

> craft eggs

> birds

Procedure:

1. Take a brown paper bag.

2. Fold the edges of the bag down (as if you were rolling up a shirt sleeve) until the bag is bowl shaped.

3. After each student has their basic nest shape, offer craft glue and an assortment of twigs, dried leaves, craft feathers and mosses to furnish the nest.

4. Encourage students to finish their nests by adhering natural materials to the inside and around the bag.

5. When finished, you may use candy eggs or craft birds to put in their nests.

TANI'S REVENGE

In the ancient time there were two brothers Tani and Taro. Tani was the elder brother and Taro was younger brother. But Tani destroyed the life of Taro. When Taro discovered the truth, he took revenge from Tani. And Tani disappeared from the native home land for many years.

But after many years Tani came back to his village. Tani secretly entered into his house through ceiling. He found that Taro was the

master of his house. Tani began to sharpen his swords to kill Taro. While sharpening his sword a drop of spit fell on the floor of the house. All the family members were sitting down. They checked the ceiling but there was no one.

But when Taro turned up to check the ceiling Tani directly attacked him but missed the target. Taro jumped down, ran around the house and cried out for help to mother earth. Taro fell into the land of witches forever.

Suddenly Tani began to repent his mistakes. He was scared of being alone on the earth. He also realized the loss of his brother. So, he kept praying day and night to all mighty God to rescue his brother Taro. God granted him a seed of peach tree towards Taro's fallen path, and asked him to recover his brother after three years. Now, Abotani was alone on earth, he was lonely and sad missing his lost brother.

Moral: *The moral of this story is that one should learn to forgive, and revenge is not the solution of any aspect of life. Revenge always leads human to remorse and degradation.*

New words

Destroy Native Witches Degradation Aspect Repent Sharpen Rescue

Reading is fun

1) What did Tani find after returning?

2) Where did Taro fall running from Tani?

3) Why did Tani keep praying after losing his brother?

4) What did God give Tani to see his brother?

Talk time

1) What is the name of your village?

2) Who is the head of your village?

3) Which would you prefer village life or town life?

4) Have you seen peaches fruit before?

Let's write

Fill in the blanks with appropriate word from the folktale.

1) Tani was __________ brother and Taro was __________ brother.

2) Tani began to __________ his brother.

3) Taro cried for __________ to the mother earth.

4) Revenge __________ the solution of any aspect of life.

Identify the words from the jumbled letters and write the word in the space provided one is done for you.

esWchit   <u>Witches</u>

erYogun   ___________   thTru   ___________

selIou   ___________   Donw   ___________

edCri   ___________   htyMig   ___________

loAne   ___________   peRent   ___________

Song time

Peaches

Peaches! Peaches! Peaches!

You look so tasty and yummy

I want to eat you all

Peaches! Peaches! Peaches!

Team Time

Activity- Stone painting

- Collect stones from the river banks

- Design and Paint on them using your imagination

Teacher's Page____ UNIT V

THEMES

- Power of an egg
- Revenge and forgiveness
- Brotherhood.

SUGGESTIONS FOR CLASSROOM TEACHING

- Read the folksong aloud with appropriate action and gesture to make it enjoyable. Ask them what they like about the folksong this will encourage the children to express themselves.

- Let the children recite the folksong along with appropriate gesture.

- You can bring a boiled egg to class. Talk to the children about the egg such as its shape, size etc. and share some amazing facts about it. Ask kids whether they like to eat egg or not. Then tell them about the nutritional values of it and how important it is to have in our regular diet.

- Read the folktale in a loud voice and focus on emphasizing the message of the folktale. At the end of the folktale reading, encourage children to tell what they have learned before you explain it. Then tell the moral of the folktale after your explanation is done.

- Explain the difficult words and new words only if they are unable to explain it.

- While teaching emphasize the importance of showing care and respect to all relations and bonding. Children should understand how important it is to protect and stand by their family.

- You can discuss with them about the various tribes in Arunachal Pradesh and their beliefs. Teach them to respects other tribes and develop a feeling of brotherhood amongst them. Explain them about "unity in diversity" and "unity is strength".

- Encourage the children to tell their tribes folktale and rituals as they have heard from their elders.

- For the bird nest activity provide each child with brown paper bag. As you instruct the children with the instructions you may join them by making the bird nest as you instruct. Help them in collecting the materials for paper craft.

- As for the stone painting activity take them to the nearest river bank and let them collect the stones in group wise as made by you. You can also arrange a small picnic party along the side of river bank and clean it after the picnic is over. Encourage them to appreciate the beauty of nature along the side of the river bank along with the importance of cleanliness.
- Encourage the children to use their own imagination and creativity on stone painting. This will help in developing their creativity.

9 7 9 8 8 9 9 8 4 3 5 9 4